5

This is my pig, Pinky.

Pinky comes when I call her by name.

"Here Pinky!"

My Farm

My Pigs

by Heather Miller

SCHOLASTIC INC.

New York   Toronto   London   Auckland   Sydney
Mexico City   New Delhi   Hong Kong   Buenos Aires

Photo Credits: Cover, p. 5, 7, 11, 13, 15, 17, 19 by Jeffrey Foxx; p. 9 © Index Stock; p. 21 © Michele Burgess/Index Stock
Contributing Editor: Jennifer Ceaser
Book Design: Michael DeLisio

Copyright © 2000 by Rosen Work Books, Inc.
All rights reserved. Published by Scholastic Inc., 555 Broadway, New York, NY 10012.
Printed in China.

ISBN 0-516-23854-X

12 13 14 15 16   62   13 12 11

Contents

Hi, I'm Ben.

Welcome to my farm.

We also have a **sow** on our farm.

A sow is a mother pig.

Her babies are called **piglets**.

Fred is our **boar**.

A boar is a father pig.

A boar is bigger than a sow.

Do you like to eat corn for breakfast?

Pigs do.

Pinky **grunts** as she eats.

13

It is a very hot day.

How do my pigs stay cool?

They lie in the mud.

15

Night is coming.

I feed my pigs one more time.

My pigs go to the **trough** to drink water.

Then it is time for them to go into their **pens**.

Goodnight, my pigs!

21

New Words

boar (**bor**) a father pig

grunts (**gruntz**) sounds a pig makes

pens (**penz**) areas where pigs sleep

piglets (**pig**-letz) baby pigs

sow (**sow**) a mother pig

trough (**trawf**) a long box that holds
  water or food

To Find Out More

Books
All Pigs are Beautiful (Read and Wonder)
by Dick King-Smith and Anita Jeram
Candlewick Press

The Three Little Pigs
by Margot Zemach
Farrar, Strauss & Giroux

Web Site
Barnyard Buddies
http://www.execpc.com/~byb/
Meet the Barnyard Buddies. Learn more about farm animals.
Includes games and posters to color. E-mail your favorite animal!

Index

About the Author
Heather Miller lives in Cambridge, Massachusetts, with her son, Jasper. She is a graduate student at Harvard University.

Reading Consultants
Kris Flynn, Coordinator, Small School District Literacy, The San Diego County Office of Education

Shelly Forys, Certified Reading Recovery Specialist, W.J. Sahnow Elementary School, Waterloo, IL

Peggy McNamara, Professor, Bank Street College of Education, Reading and Literacy Program